JOHN LENNON for UKULELE

Cover photo courtesy Photofest

ISBN 978-1-4950-0684-5

HAL•LEONARD®
CORPORATION
7777 W. BLUEMOUND RD. P.O. BOX 13819 MILWAUKEE, WI 53213

Visit Hal Leonard Online at
www.halleonard.com

Beautiful Boy
(Darling Boy)

Words and Music by John Lennon

Bridge

Yes, it's a long _____ way to go, but in the mean -

- time...   3. Be - fore you cross the street, _

take my hand. _   Life is what hap - pens to

you while you're bus - y mak - ing oth - er plans. _

Outro-Chorus

Beau - ti - ful, beau - ti - ful, beau - ti - ful, beau - ti - ful boy. _

Dar - ling, dar - ling, dar - ling, dar - ling Sean. _

Imagine

Words and Music by John Lennon

(Instrumental)

1. I-mag-ine there's no heav-en, it's eas-y if you try; __ __ no hell __ be-low us, a-bove us on-ly sky. __ I-mag-ine all the peo-ple __ liv-ing for to-day, __ ah. __

Verse

2. I - mag - ine there's no coun - tries,
3. *See additional lyrics*

it is - n't hard _____ to do; _____

noth - ing to kill or die _____ for

and no re - li - gion, too. _____

I - mag - ine all the peo - ple _____

liv - ing life in peace. _____ You, _____

6

Chorus

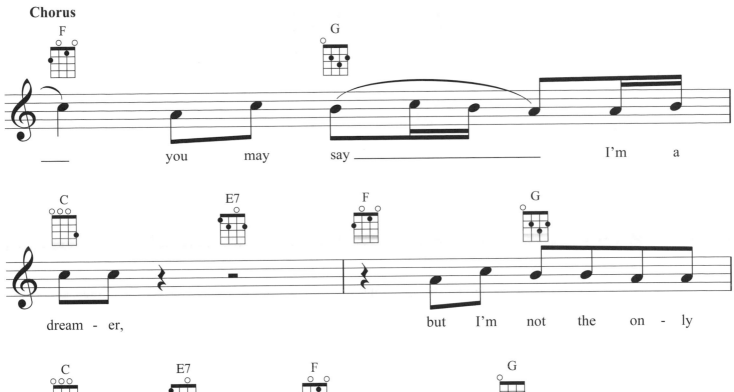

you may say _____ I'm a dream-er, but I'm not the on - ly one. I hope some day _____ you'll join us _____ and the world _____ will

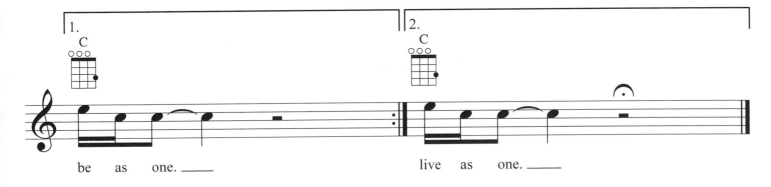

1. be as one. _____

2. live as one. _____

Additional Lyrics

3. Imagine no possessions,
I wonder if you can;
No need for greed or hunger,
A brotherhood of man.
Imagine all the people sharing all the world.

Cold Turkey

Words and Music by John Lennon

First note

Verse
Moderate Rock

Am

1. Tem - p'ra - ture's ris - ing, fe - ver is high. ___
(2., 3.) *See additional lyrics*

Can't see no fu - ture, can't see no sky. ___

My feet are so heav - y, so is my head. ___

I wish I was a ba - by. I

Chorus
C

wish I was dead. ___ Cold tur - key ___ has

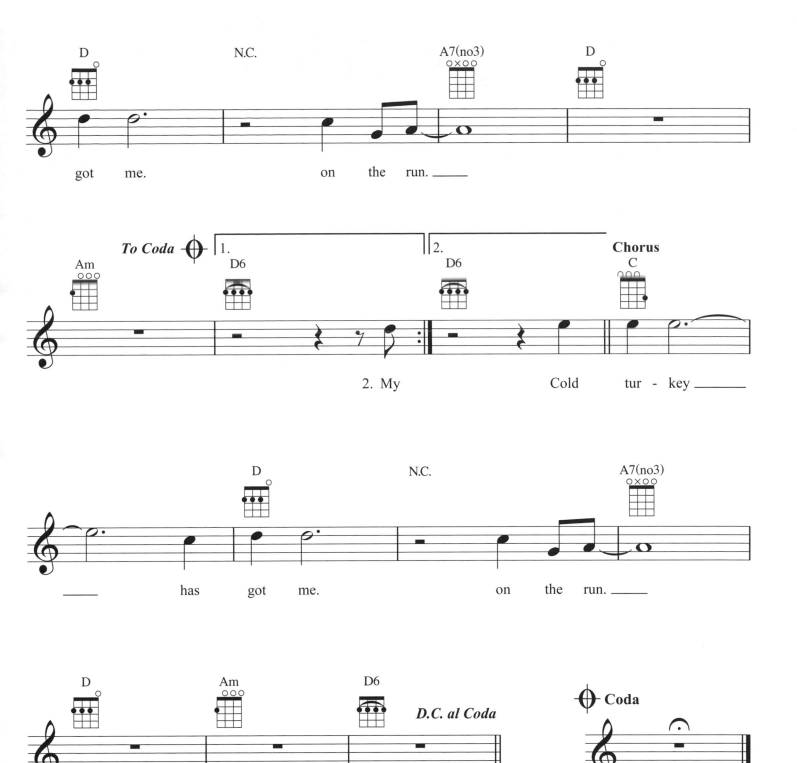

Additional Lyrics

2. My body is aching, goosepimple bone.
   Can't see nobody; leave me alone.
   My eyes are wide open, can't get to sleep.
   One thing I'm sure of:
   I'm in at the deep freeze.

3. Thirty-six hours rolling in pain,
   Praying to someone: free me again.
   Oh, I'll be a good boy; please make me well.
   I promise you anything;
   Get me out of this hell.

Give Peace a Chance

Words and Music by John Lennon

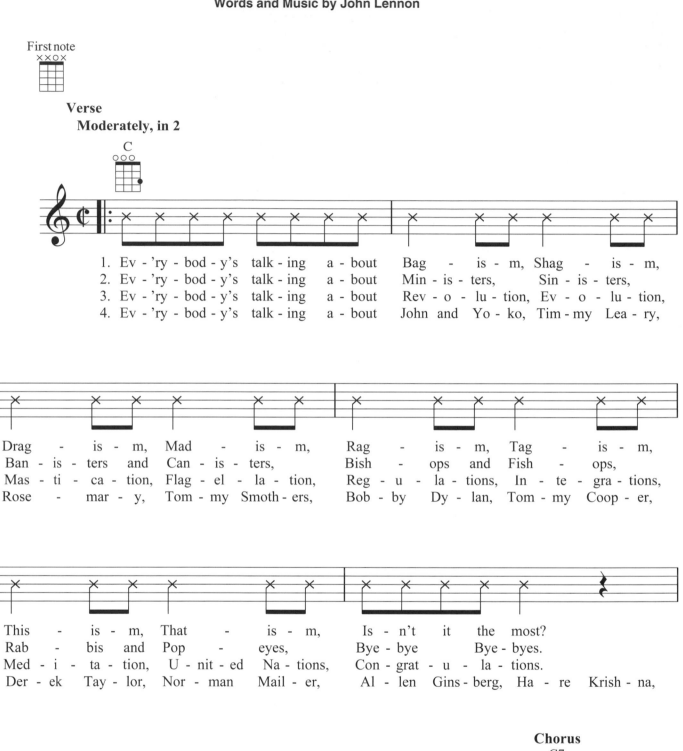

First note

Verse
Moderately, in 2

1. Ev-'ry-bod-y's talk-ing a-bout Bag-is-m, Shag-is-m,
2. Ev-'ry-bod-y's talk-ing a-bout Min-is-ters, Sin-is-ters,
3. Ev-'ry-bod-y's talk-ing a-bout Rev-o-lu-tion, Ev-o-lu-tion,
4. Ev-'ry-bod-y's talk-ing a-bout John and Yo-ko, Tim-my Lea-ry,

Drag-is-m, Mad-is-m, Rag-is-m, Tag-is-m,
Ban-is-ters and Can-is-ters, Bish-ops and Fish-ops,
Mas-ti-ca-tion, Flag-el-la-tion, Reg-u-la-tions, In-te-gra-tions,
Rose-mar-y, Tom-my Smoth-ers, Bob-by Dy-lan, Tom-my Coop-er,

This-is-m, That-is-m, Is-n't it the most?
Rab-bis and Pop-eyes, Bye-bye Bye-byes.
Med-i-ta-tion, U-nit-ed Na-tions, Con-grat-u-la-tions.
Der-ek Tay-lor, Nor-man Mail-er, Al-len Gins-berg, Ha-re Krish-na,

Chorus
G7

Ha-re, Ha-re Krish-na.

All we ___ are say -

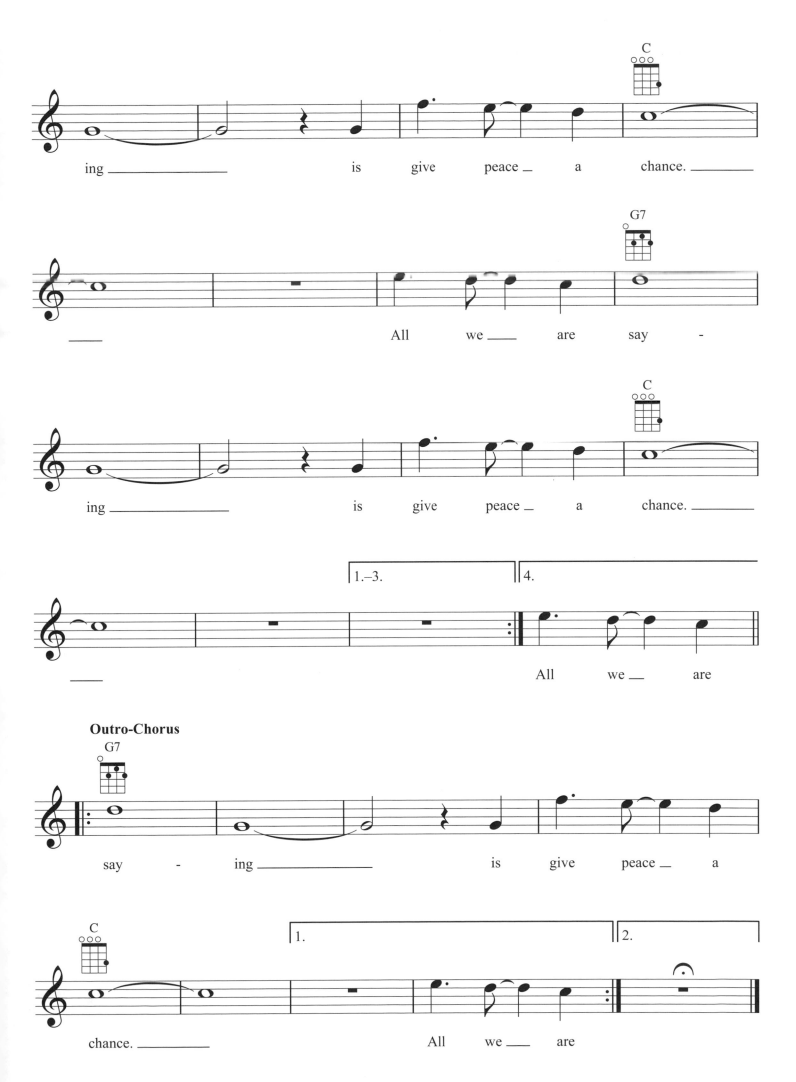

ing _____ is give peace __ a chance. _____

____ All we __ are say -

ing _____ is give peace __ a chance. _____

1.–3. **4.**

____ All we __ are

Outro-Chorus

say - ing _____ is give peace __ a

1. **2.**

chance. _____ All we __ are

Grow Old with Me

Words and Music by John Lennon

Additional Lyrics

2. Grow old along with me,
   Two branches of one tree.
   Face the setting sun
   When the day is done.
   God bless our love,
   God bless our love.

3. Grow old along with me,
   Whatever fate decrees.
   We will see it through,
   For our love is true.
   God bless our love,
   God bless our love.

Happy Xmas
(War Is Over)
Written by John Lennon and Yoko Ono

Additional Lyrics

2. And so, this is Xmas for weak and for strong,
   The rich and the poor ones; the road is so long.
   And so, happy Xmas for black and for white,
   For the yellow and red ones; let's stop all the fights.

3. And so, this is Xmas, and what have we done?
   Another year over, a new one just begun.
   And so, happy Xmas; we hope you have fun,
   The near and the dear ones, the old and the young.

Instant Karma

Words and Music by John Lennon

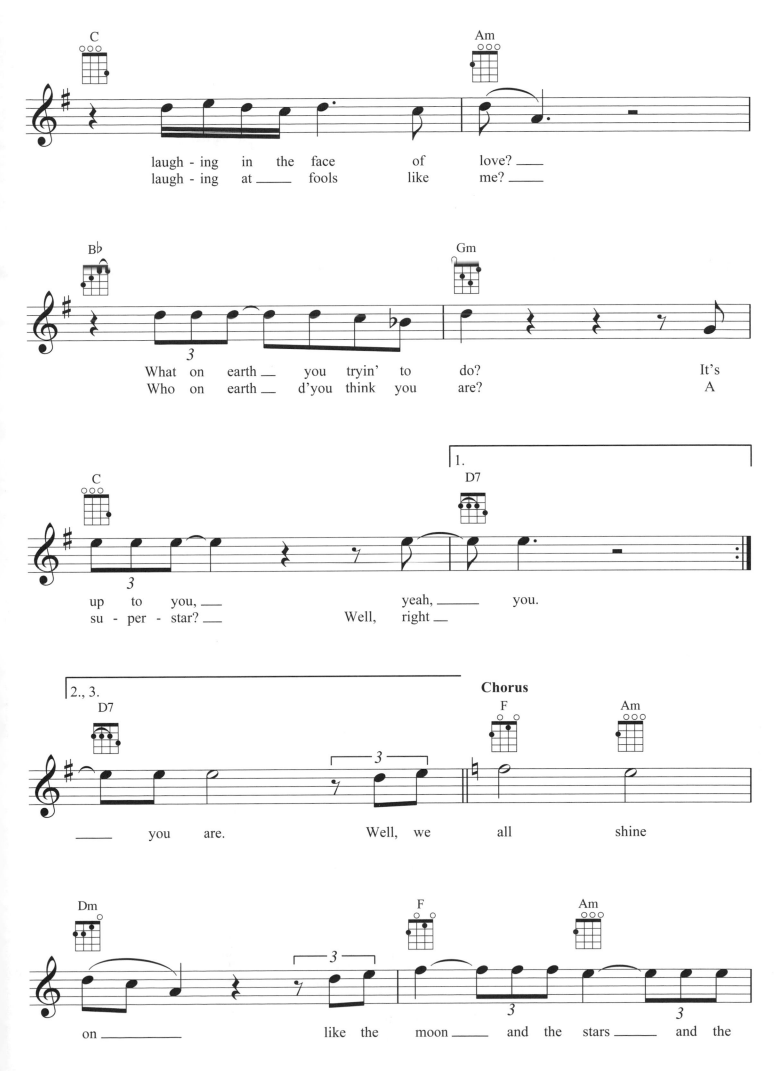

laugh - ing in the face of love? ____
laugh - ing at ____ fools like me? ____

What on earth ____ you tryin' to do? It's
Who on earth ____ d'you think you are? A

1.

up to you, ____ yeah, ____ you.
su - per - star? ____ Well, right ____

2., 3.

Chorus

____ you are. Well, we all shine

on ____ like the moon ____ and the stars ____ and the

Additional Lyrics

3. Instant karma's gonna get you,
   Gonna knock you off your feet.
   Better recognize your brothers;
   Everyone you meet.
   Why in the world are we here?
   Surely not to live in pain and fear.
   Why on earth are you there
   When you're everywhere?
   Come and get your share.

Nobody Told Me

Words and Music by John Lennon

§ Verse

al - ways some - thing hap - p'ning and noth - ing go - ing on. _____ There's
4. Ev - 'ry - bod - y's fly - ing and no one leaves the ground. _ Well,
5. Ev - 'ry - bod - y's smok - ing and no one's get - ting high. _____

al - ways some - thing cook - ing and noth - ing in the pot. _____ They're
ev - 'ry - bod - y's cry - ing and no one makes a sound. _ There's a
Ev - 'ry - bod - y's fly - ing and nev - er touch the sky. _____ There's

starv - ing back in Chi - na, so fin - ish what you got. _____
place for us in mov - ies; you just got - ta lay a - round. _
U - F - Os o - ver New York and I ain't too sur - prised. _

Interlude

(Instrumental)

Chorus

No - bod - y told me there'd be days like

20

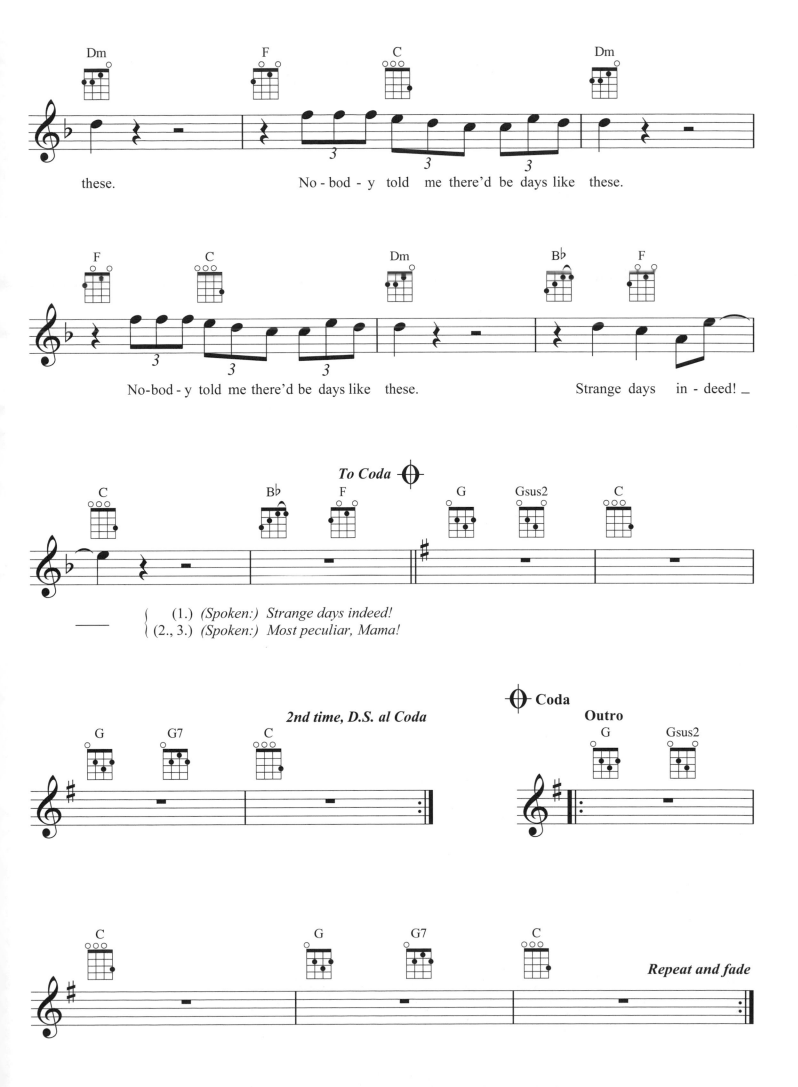

these.

No - bod - y told me there'd be days like these.

No-bod - y told me there'd be days like these.

Strange days in - deed! _

To Coda

(1.) (Spoken:) Strange days indeed!
(2., 3.) (Spoken:) Most peculiar, Mama!

2nd time, D.S. al Coda

Coda

Outro

Repeat and fade

Jealous Guy

Words and Music by John Lennon

Additional Lyrics

2. I was feeling insecure,
   You might not love me anymore.
   I was shivering inside,
   I was shivering inside.

3. *Whistle melody*

4. I was trying to catch your eyes,
   Thought that you was trying to hide.
   I was swallowing my pain,
   I was swallowing my pain.

Look at Me

Written by John Lennon

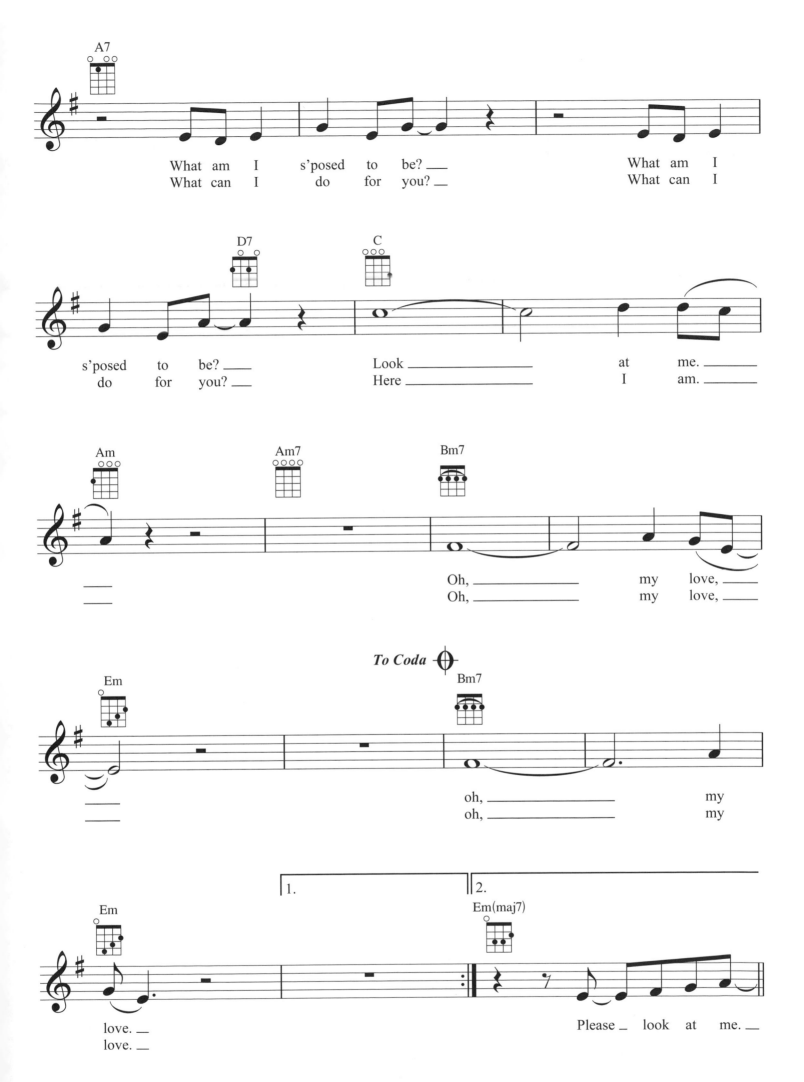

Additional Lyrics

3. Who am I?
   Nobody knows but me.
   Nobody knows but me.
   Who am I?
   Nobody else can see,
   Just you and me.
   Who are we?
   Oh, my love, oh, my love.

#9 Dream

Words and Music by John Lennon

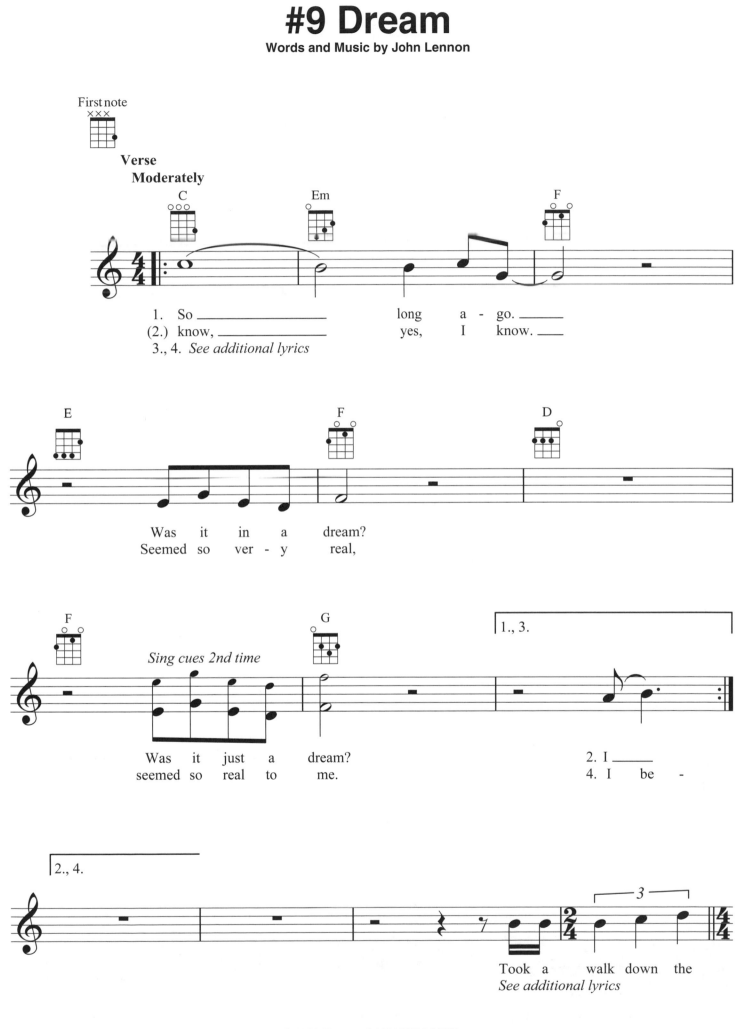

Pre-Chorus

street.

Through the heat whis-pered trees.

I thought I could hear,

hear,

hear, —

hear

some-bod-y call out my

name *(Spoken:)* John... as it start-ed to ___ rain.

Chorus

Two spir-its danc-ing so strange.

Ah, ___ bö-wa-ka-

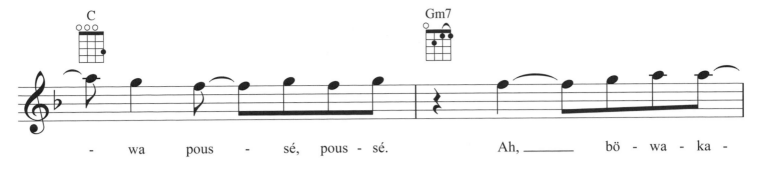

- wa pous - sé, pous - sé. Ah, _____ bö - wa - ka -

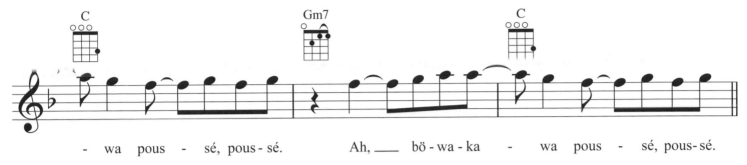

- wa pous - sé, pous - sé. Ah, ___ bö - wa - ka - wa pous - sé, pous - sé.

Interlude

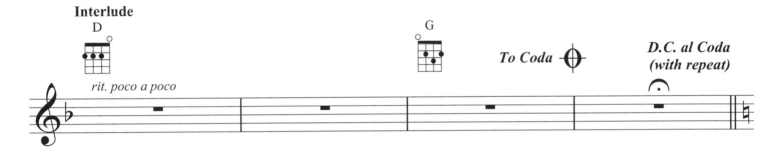

rit. poco a poco

To Coda ⊕

D.C. al Coda (with repeat)

⊕ **Coda**

Outro-Chorus

Repeat and fade

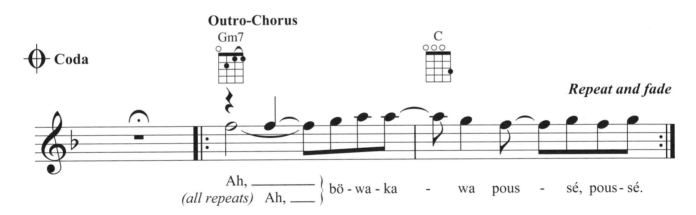

Ah, _____
(all repeats) Ah, ___ } bö - wa - ka - wa pous - sé, pous - sé.

Additional Lyrics

3. Dream, dream away.
   Magic in the air.
   Was magic in the air?

4. I believe, yes, I believe.
   More I cannot say.
   What more can I say?

Pre-Chorus: On a river of sound
Through the mirror go 'round, 'round.
I thought I could feel, feel, feel, feel
Music touching my soul,
Something warm, sudden cold.
The spirit dance was unfolding.

Love

Words and Music by John Lennon

Mind Games

Words and Music by John Lennon

-id dudes ___ lift-ing the veil, ___ do-ing the

mind _____ guer - ril - la. Some call it mag-

- ic, the search for the grail.

Bridge

Love is the an - swer, _____ and

Yes is the an - swer, _____ and

you know that for sure. ___

you know that for sure. ___

Love _____ is a flow - er; _____ you

Yes _____ is sur - ren - der; _____ you

Mother

Words and Music by John Lennon

1. Moth - er, _____ you had me but I nev - er had
2. Fa - ther, _____ you left me but I nev - er left
3. Chil - dren, _____ don't __ do what I __ have

you. _____
you. _____
done. _____

I _____ want - ed you; _____ you did - n't want
I _____ need - ed you; _____ you did - n't need
I _____ could - n't walk _____ and I tried to

me.
me.
run.

So __ I, _____

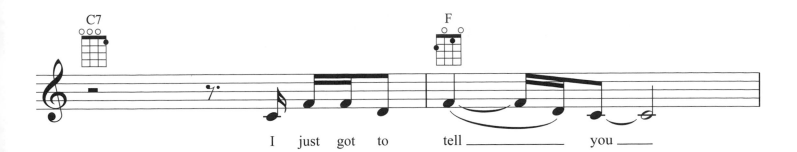

I just got to tell _____ you ____

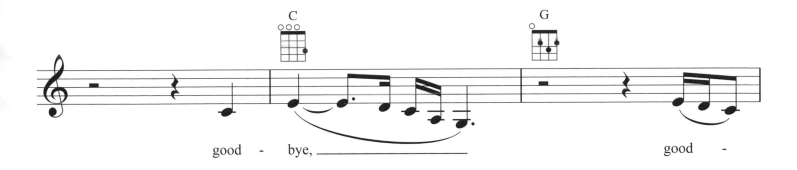

good - bye, _____ good -

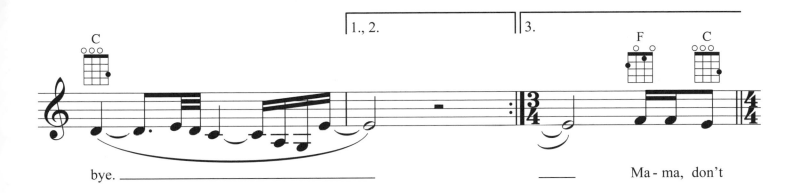

bye. _____ ____ Ma - ma, don't

Outro

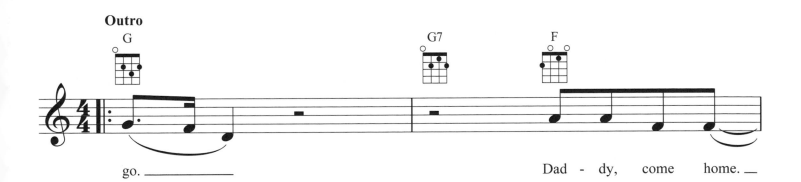

go. ____ Dad - dy, come home. __

Repeat and fade

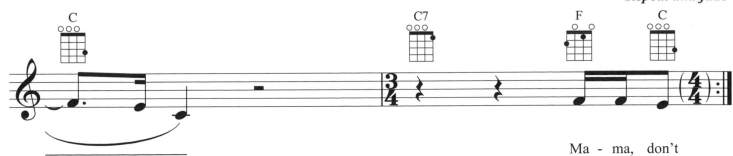

Ma - ma, don't

Power to the People

Words and Music by John Lennon

First note

Intro-Chorus
Moderate Gospel Rock

N.C.

Pow-er to the peo - ple, pow-er to the peo-

Chorus

D   Em7   D

- ple. Pow - er to the peo - ple,

Em7   D   Em7

pow - er to the peo - ple, pow - er to the peo-

To Coda

D   Cmaj7   D

- ple, pow - er to the peo - ple, right on. _____

1. You
2. A mil - lion
3. I got to

Verse

Em7

say you want a rev - o - lu - tion, we'd bet - ter
work - ers work - in' for noth - ing, you bet - ter
ask you, com - rades and broth - ers, how do you

get   on   right   a - way. _____   Well, let's get
give   them what   they   real - ly   own. _____   We   got   to
treat your   old   wom - an   back home? _____   She's   got   to

1., 2.

on   your   feet, ___   and   in - to   the   street, __   sing - ing:
put   you   down __   when we   come   in - to _____   town, __   sing - ing:
be   her - self ___   so   she   can

3.   *D.S. al Coda*   ⊕ **Coda**

D

give   us ___   help, __   sing - ing: _____

Outro-Chorus

D   Em7   D   Em7

Pow - er   to   the   peo - ple,   pow - er   to   the   peo -

D   Em7   D

- ple,   pow - er   to   the   peo - ple,

Cmaj7   D   *Repeat and fade*

pow - er   to   the   peo - ple,   right   on. _____

(Just Like)
Starting Over

Words and Music by John Lennon

2. Ev -’ry

Why don’t we take off a -

Bridge

lone, __

take a trip some - where far, far a - way? __

We’ll be to - geth - er all a - lone _____ a -

gain,

like we used to ____ in the ear - ly days. __

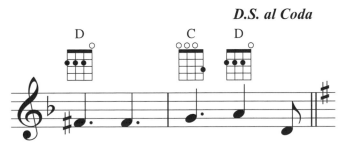

D.S. al Coda

Well, well, dar - lin’. 3. It’s

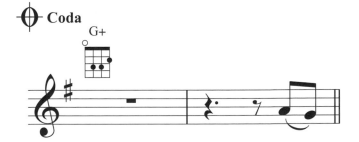

Coda

Our __

Outro

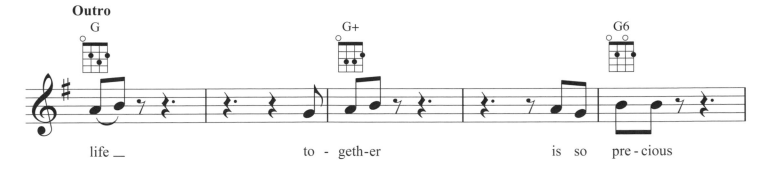

life __

to - geth - er

is so pre - cious

to - geth- er.   We have grown. ___

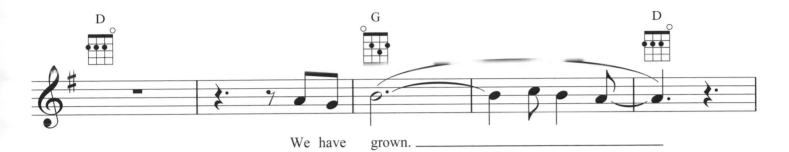

We have grown. _____

Al - though our love   is still spe - cial,

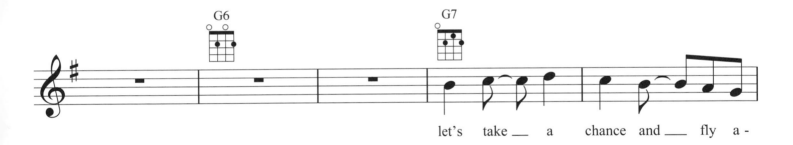

let's take ___ a   chance and ___ fly a -

way ___   some - where. _____

Repeat and fade

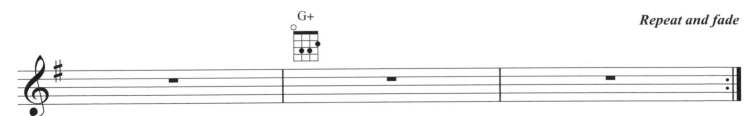

Watching the Wheels

Words and Music by John Lennon

1. Peo-ple say I'm cra-zy
2. Peo-ple say I'm la-zy,
3. Peo-ple ask-ing ques-tions,

do-in' what I'm do - in'. ___
dream-in' my life ___ a - way. ___
lost in con - fu - sion. ___

Well, they give me all kinds ___ of warn -
Well, they give me all kinds ___ of ad -
Well, I tell them there's ___ no prob -

- ings   to save me from
- vice   de - signed to en -
- lem,   on - ly so -

C

ru - in. _____
light - en me. _____   When I
lu - tions. _____   Well, they

Pre-Chorus

F   **Dm**   **G**

When I   say that I'm _____   o - kay, _____   well, they   look at me kind - a strange: _____
tell 'em   that I'm do - in'   fine _____   watch-ing   shad - ows on _____ the wall, _____
shake their   heads and they   look at me _____   as   if   I've lost _____ my mind. _____

F   **Dm**

_____   "Sure - ly you're _ not hap - py now; _ you no
_____   "Don't you miss _ the big _____ time, boy? _ You're no
_____   I   tell them there's _ no hur - ry; I'm _____ just

G   1.

long - er play _ the game." _____
long - er on _ the ball." _____
sit - ing here do - ing time. _____

2., 3.

45

Interlude

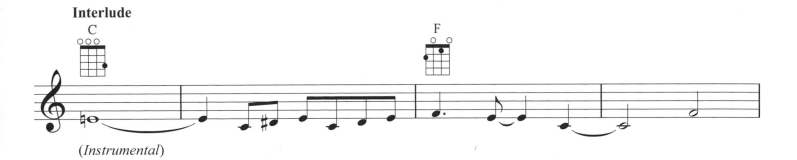

(Instrumental)

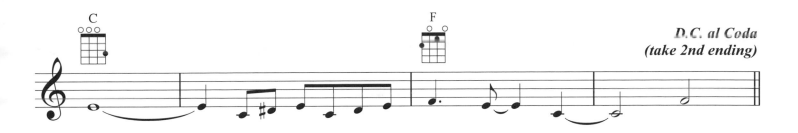

D.C. al Coda
(take 2nd ending)

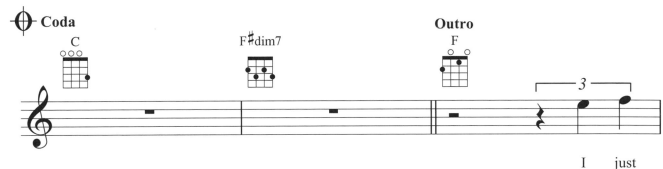

Coda

Outro

I   just

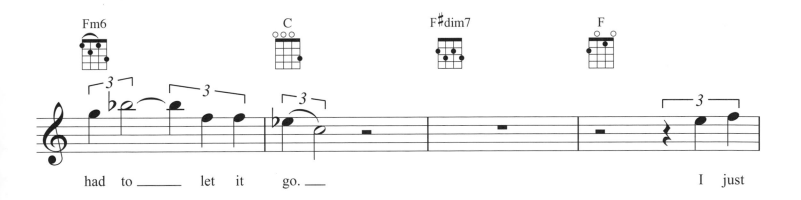

had   to _____ let   it   go. ___

I   just

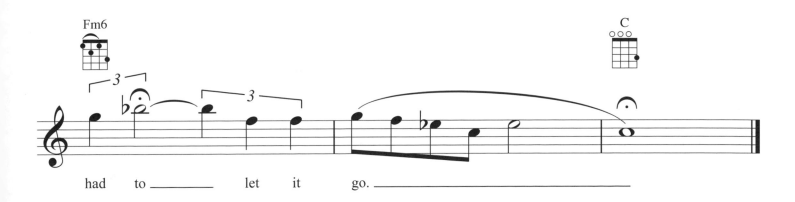

had   to _____ let   it   go. _____

Whatever Gets You Through the Night

Words and Music by John Lennon

Don't need a sword to cut thru flow - ers, ___
Don't need a watch to waste your time, ___
Don't need a gun to blow your mind, ___

oh no, ___ oh no. ___

1.
What - ev - er gets ___ you thru your

2., 3.

Interlude

Hold me, dar - lin'. Come on, lis - ten to ___ me.

49

I won't do _____ you no harm.

Trust me, dar - lin'. Come on, lis - ten to _____ me. Come on,

lis - ten to _____ me. Come on, lis - ten, lis - ten.

Interlude

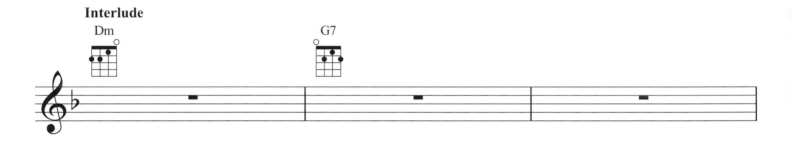

To Coda

D.S. al Coda
(take 2nd ending)

Coda

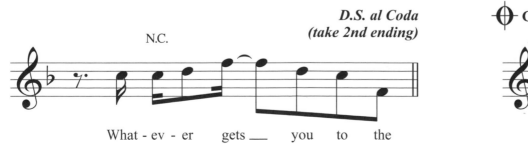

What - ev - er gets ___ you to the

Woman

Words and Music by John Lennon

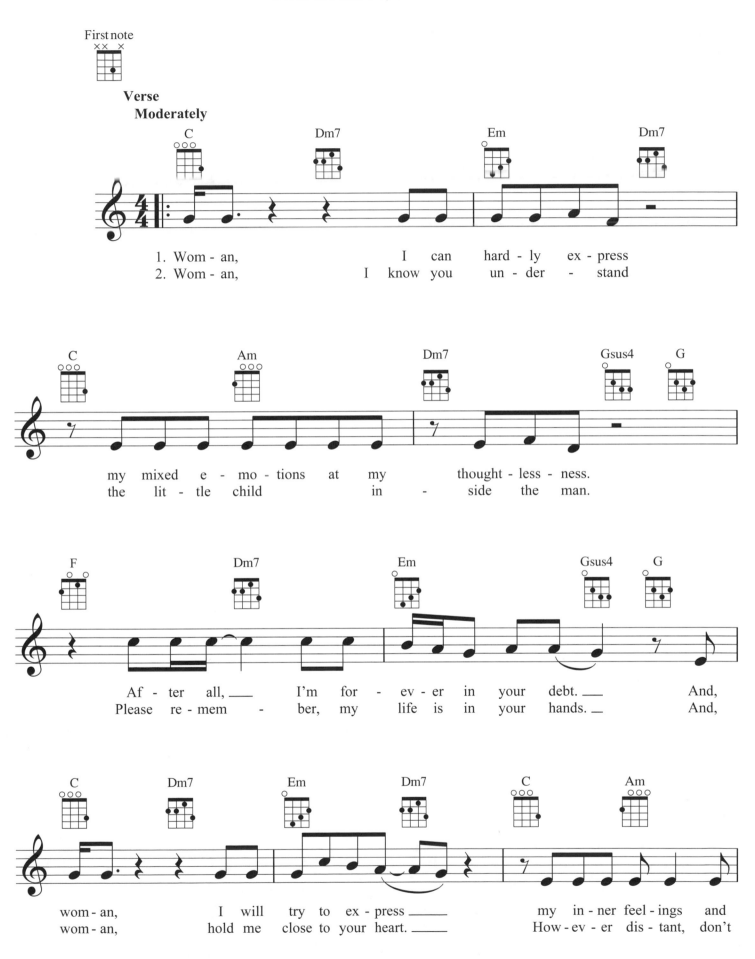

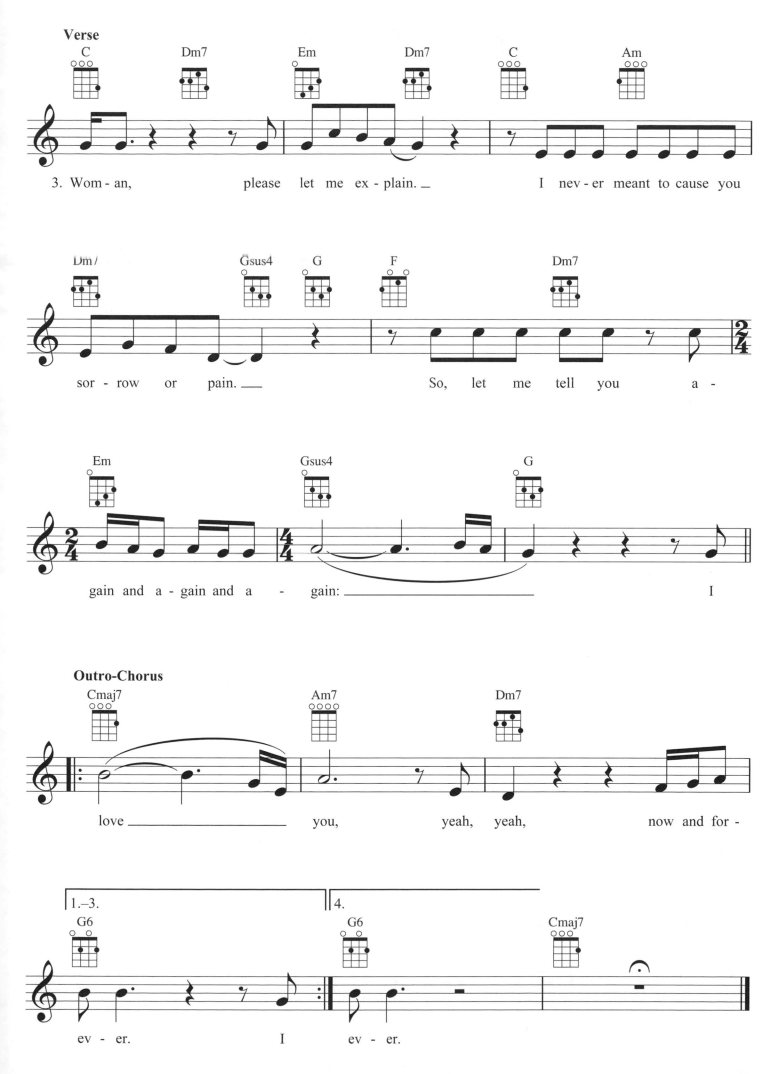

Working Class Hero

Words and Music by John Lennon

Let chords ring till end.

Additional Lyrics

2. They've hurt you at home and they hit you at school.
   They hate you if you're clever and they despise a fool,
   Till you're so f**king crazy you can't follow their rules.

3. When they've tortured and scared you for twenty odd years,
   Then they expect you to pick a career
   When you can't really function you're so full of fear.

4. Keep you doped with religion and sex and TV,
   And you think you're so clever and classless and free.
   But you're still f**king peasants, as far as I can see.

5. "There's room at the top," they are telling you still,
   "But first, you must learn how to smile as you kill
   If you want to be like the folks on the hill."